SERVICE

Category: Business & Economics

Description: How to give more service and help customers build their business. This is one of 13 books based on Benjamin Franklin's 13-week self improvement program (Ben Franklin's 13 virtues) that will help you build your customer's business by giving extra service. After reading this eBook and focusing on your primary goal for one week of giving your customers extra service and helping them become more successful your customer relationships will improve starting immediately. You are not just selling products and services they can buy from any competitor, you will be selling them ideas, consulting as well as add on services.

Key words: service and success, attitude of service, customer service attitude, improve customer service, customer service skills, better customer service, customer service improvement, Ben Franklin's 13-virtues

ISBN 978-1-105-22675-5

Written and published by Bob Oros
832 NW 142nd Street, Edmond, OK 73013
405-751-9191 Email Bob@BobOros.com
Web site www.BobOros.com

ISBN 978-1-105-22675-5 90000

9 781105 226755

Service

Help customers build their business

Key to selling anybody

How would you like to KNOW with absolute certainty that you could sell anybody? What if you had a magic key that would open the door to everyone you called on? You can! And once you know the secret formula - and apply it - your sales will take off!

You will lose all feelings of call reluctance. Your confidence will double - or even triple. Your income will increase. You will have everything you ever wanted in life.

Here it is...

Find out by careful listening and questioning what your customer wants and let them know that you are sincerely interested in helping them get it.

Too simple? Let's try it on YOU. What do you want most in life. Do you want more cash? A new home? Money in the bank? Financial security?

Now, what if someone came into your life who was sincerely interested in helping you get those things? What if they went out of their way to show you how to increase your income? What if they helped you find ways to save and invest more of the money you work so hard to make so you could become financially secure? What if they helped you find and buy the home of your dreams? Would you want to know this person a little better?

On the other hand what if another person came into your life and all they wanted to do was sell you what THEY thought you should have? If they were overly aggressive, pushy, wanted to get you to do things you were not really interested in - how would you react? Do you see the difference? Wouldn't it feel good to have someone who is sincerely interested in helping you succeed?

I know what you are thinking - the only person who is that interested in ME is my mother! Remember, this is not about YOU - it is about selling - it is about your customer. Don't EXPECT anyone to be that interested in you. But that doesn't mean you cannot be that interested and helpful to your customers. This changes the whole focus.

Now I am going to show YOU how to make any amount of money you want by using this theory. You see, I AM interested in your success - I want you to sell more and make more money.

Let's say you want to make $120,000 over the next 12 months. Normally you would say to yourself - "THIS IS MY GOAL - I WILL MAKE $120,000 IN COMMISSIONS DURING THE NEXT 12 MONTHS." By taking this approach your focus is wrong.

Instead, try this... "I AM GOING TO GIVE $500 WORTH OF SERVICE EVERY DAY MONDAY THROUGH FRIDAY." Do you see the difference? Don't focus on

the money - on what's in it for YOU - focus on GIVING
THE SERVICE. The money will follow.

This is the new definition of selling - service. This
definition is so new it is not even in the dictionary or
thesaurus. The dictionary says selling means to
persuade, or influence to a course of action. The
thesaurus says selling is "barter, exchange, trade, traffic,
and vend. Nowhere does it say selling is SERVICE.
Nowhere does it say selling is helping your customers
become more successful and make more money.

Let's put it another way. How much would someone PAY
YOU to listen to your sales pitch. Zero - Right? Yet
people pay thousands of dollars to consultants to ask
questions - find out what they want - and help them get it.
You can convey the same message to your customers.
The true purpose of a consultative sales person is to find
out what your customer wants and help them get it.

To accomplish this you have to listen more that you talk.
If you can get your customer to talk enough, they simply
cannot disguise their real goals and real motives. They

may try as hard as they can, but invariably they will "give themselves away". When they do - you have the key.

YOU KNOW WHAT THEY WANT!

Help them get it and you will have captured the true meaning of being a sales professional.

Building relationships

What has caused you, in the past, to think about the possibility of doing something besides selling? Here is the answer. The indifferent, reluctant, defensive attitude that greets you every time you make a sales call is what defeats nearly everyone who fails in a selling career.

Wouldn't it be nice if you were welcomed everywhere you went? If potential customers said "yes, come in, tell me more?"

What can you do or say that will make a prospect treat you favorably? How can you get them to change from indifference and reluctance to being receptive and looking at your products and services?

Here is the answer. Changing their attitude starts by controlling your attitude. You have to continue to feel good about them even if they don't feel good about you, or themselves.

Not as easy as it sounds. Keep in mind that you are not selling products and services, you are selling yourself.

If your company comes out with a new product you can be sure every competitor is finding out how it can be duplicated. The same goes for services. Come out with a new way of providing extra services and you will have an edge for a while. However, it won't be long before a competitor will be offering the same service.

Adding extra services without increasing your price is actually lowering your gross profit. As one president of a large distribution company said, "All I really have is a warehouse full of commodities."

If the difference is the personal relationship you can establish with your customers, what can you do to enhance that relationship? To answer this question all you have to do is ask what makes you like or dislike someone you are doing business with.

You like people who like you. Someone who is interested in all aspects of your business. Someone who talks about the things you want and the goals you are trying to accomplish.

Here is the secret of getting past their indifference. Here is what would make YOU buy from someone. When someone has the tools to help you succeed and their main purpose is to provide those tools for your use and help you achieve your goals, it is impossible not to feel the desire to work with them.

Let's say that again... it is important.

When someone has the tools to help YOU succeed and their main purpose is to provide those tools for YOUR use and help YOU achieve YOUR goals, it is IMPOSSIBLE not to feel the desire to work with them.

Most of the time customers and prospects don't know what they want. You, as a sales consultant, have to help your customers identify their goals and show them you are interested in helping them succeed.

Sounds altruistic, I know. But consider this - as one very successful sales person put it when asked why he did so much for his customers, why he always went the extra mile and always put his customers first; "because I am a very selfish person. I like to make money."

Another benefit of this "altruistic" approach - it gets your mind off of yourself and you lose your fear.

Why they are out of business

"Doing business based on relationships, service, and trust, is just not as highly valued as it used to be."

"In today's economy it has become about contracts and pennies."

"The passion for service is gone."

"Willing to do what-ever-it-takes to serve the customer doesn't have the value it used to have."

Those are four quotes from the president of a distribution company given during an interview as the reason they shut down their business.

I have some concerns about this. As bad as I hate to see anyone close down (because it can almost always be avoided) I think these reasons are pretty thin.

Let's do a little case study. Let's look at this from the customer's point of view.

Relationship:

If you think relationships are not highly valued, try doing business without one. Just the opposite is true!

I am not going to pay a higher price because of our relationship, but you will get to keep my business if we have a good relationship and you don't take advantage of it. I mean that when your company has a special price on something and you don't offer it to me because you know I will buy it anyway, is that a relationship or are you just using me to pad your gross profit?

If a competitor comes in and offers me a lower price on something that you have been overcharging me on, is that taking a relationship seriously? It seems to me that a relationship is a two way street. I give you my business and you take care of me.

I have every competitor in the market calling on me begging for my business? Do you think I am going to turn them away while you are calling me on the phone for your order and they are bringing me samples, specials and ideas?

From a customer's point of view the relationship has to be stronger than ever before. It has to be sincere. It has to be beneficial for both of us.

Trust: Integrity is another word for trust. Do these examples below make me trust you? You can fool some of the people some of the time, but trust is more important than ever. You have to earn it by telling the truth.

Do these examples build trust?

A pound cake is not really a pound.

A foot long hot dog is only 10 inches.

Many number 10 cans are not number 10's.

Shrimp baskets don't have all the shrimp.

Retailers put incorrect prices in their scanners.

Product manipulation, product substitution and short weight are considered strategies.

Intentional invoice over charges and mistakes are built into the system of many banks, credit card companies and mortgage companies.

Water is injected in lobster tails to increase their weight.

Products are in the market that are over breaded, over glazed and over pumped.

Scallops are soaked in sodium-trypoly-phosphate to increase weight.

37 billion bottles of water are sold every year with much of it being simply tap water!

HONESTY ALWAYS WORKS BEST! The best sales person is always the one who bluntly tells the truth. It is not only impressive but it leaves a trail of trust behind. Not the best talker wins, it's the most honest talker. The best approach to building customer trust is to deserve confidence.

Service: "What-ever-it-takes to serve the customer doesn't have the value it used to have!" Immediate, enthusiastic and energetic response to a customer request is more valued than ever.

The problem is sales people have become so dependent on technology that the secret of good customer service has disappeared! What does your voice mail sound like? If you are a president or vice president, call your own company and see what impression your customers are getting. Passion for service is more appreciated than it has ever been, because it is so rare!

"Dial 1 for shipping, dial 2 for warehouse, dial 3 for directions, dial 4 for credit, dial 5 for accounts payable!" Is that "what-ever-it-takes service?"

Here's the bottom line. Things are changing. FAST. And if you are not changing with them you know what will happen.

The solution? You have to do things the hard way - you have to go back to SELLING! You have to get back to making face to face contact (that's called service), bring your customers VALUE and some good reasons to TRUST you so you can build a good relationship.

Your customers are smart

Your customers are smarter than you think they are. They realize that you can't be all things to all people. When you are honest about what you can't do the trust they have in you goes up.

Here is an example.

A test was conducted on the advertising of five products. They ran two ads - one that said they had superiority in all five products and another ad that claimed superiority in three of the five. Which one do you think did better? The advertisement that exposed their weakness did much better.

Why? Customers have become numb to selling pitches and marketing that promises miracle cures. When you make a statement like "this may not be the product for you" your credibility has increased. The customer has more trust in you.

I know. I know. This sounds like to old joke about the sales person who says "you don't want to buy anything today, do you?" This is different. This is admitting that you can't deliver the moon. This is being honest. This is building trust. And people will only buy from people they trust!

When you honestly state a weakness, you are actually helping your customer make a good decision. They will believe you when you tell them what you CAN do.

The advertisement used by Chevy is a good example. Chevy compares itself with Honda and says they are superior in five models except one. Chevy does not make lawn mowers and Honda does. In their example they use it with humor, however, I don't think they realize how powerful the technique could be if they used it with a tone of seriousness. The fact that Chevy could be big enough to admit that they are highly superior in certain models while admitting that they are not the leader in one or two categories (with justifiable reasons) their believability would be higher.

When there is even a small doubt in your mind about whether the product is right for them, let your customer know. Let the customer know you will be personally checking to make sure that your product does the job and the customer is happy with the purchase.

Remember, you can't sell anybody anything. The harder you try the more the resistance goes up.

What you CAN do is help them make a good decision. You want your customer for the long haul, not just the immediate sale that will come back to bite you. Especially if you over promise and under deliver.

As a professional speaker, I have turned down plenty of opportunities because I didn't feel I was the right fit. Of course I had to learn this the hard way. I teach sales negotiating. How to make more money by giving more value. I once accepted a speaking engagement for a government agency that really didn't understand the profit concept. Needless to say, I didn't connect with the audience. I now know better. It is not worth the paycheck when you leave knowing that you blew it.

So when something comes along that is not a good fit, I
let them know and they have much more faith and trust
in me. Somehow turning it down always seems to come
back in good way.

I can't teach the government how to make better deals,
but I can sure teach YOU how to increase your sales and
profits in these challenging times.

A Faster Horse

When Henry Ford asked his customers what they needed they said "A faster horse!"

If you're asking your customers what they need what will they tell you? "Cheaper prices!"

Henry Ford could see beyond the immediate obvious, look into the future and see a bigger picture. And that is what you must do to have record breaking sales.

Let's go one step further. What do YOU need? If your answer is more sales, more customers and more money, you are giving the same answer as a "A faster horse!" You are not looking at the bigger picture. You are not looking beyond the immediate obvious. You are not focusing on what will create your increased sales.

What you really need is to put tons of extra value in every product and service you offer.

And exactly how do you do that? By improving the level of service that is included with your price. Because when all things are equal, which is most of the time, the difference will be in the extra personal service you provide.

If you are not sure what good service is, here's a short summary. This is an outline of what I present in my customer service seminar that will add value to every product and service you sell:

ATTITUDE Everyone has bad days, however, you must take control by applying this little know technique: ACT like you are having a good day and your attitude will follow. Wipe that scowl off your face and replace it with a genuine smile. Put a little energy in the way you move around and like magic, you will begin to feel better. And so will your customer. An attitude of "what-ever-it-takes-service" is what you really need. Being an example of what it really means.

APPRECIATION 25% of your customers will leave you for a competitor this year. The biggest reason? You didn't let them know how much you really appreciate their business. You didn't take the time to invest that little extra thank you! Nothing is more appreciated than a little sincere appreciation. If it comes right down to a decision between buying from you and buying from a competitor, something as small as an attitude of appreciation will often times tip the scale in your favor.

ATTENTION To be different and really stand out PAY ATTENTION and watch the immediate difference it makes. For example, out of the thousands of hotels I have stayed in only ONE noticed that my email address was also a website address. The young man behind the counter greeted me and said "I see you are a motivational speaker." I was shocked that he took the time to visit my website. People are so preoccupied with themselves they rarely take time to actually be interested in another person.

ACTION "Do it now" is not just a cute little phrase, it is the best compliment you can possibly give a customer: immediate response to their problem. Adopt the philosophy of taking care of business NOW and watch your customers say WOW!

So what you really need is not a faster horse or cheaper prices. You need to be MOTIVATED to improve your service to your customers. And what could be newer and more welcome to your customers than a motivated, excited sales person delivering great service. It has been missing for the past several years. Everyone has been taking their customers for granted. Ho Hum! Selling is dead and if you are still delivering it, you too will be dead.

Instead of saying I need more sales, more customers and more money, try saying I need to GIVE more. I need to give my customers an enthusiastic attitude of service, more appreciation, more attention and more action!

Try implementing my "Straight 'A' Service" principles for a while and you will get to your objective a lot faster, but it wont be with a faster horse. It will be with a 4 X 4 supped up vehicle called Attitude-Appreciation-Attention-Action.

Make more calls

A marketing company did a direct mail campaign to homes in a large city making a special price offer on a product and kept track of the results. They mailed to 50,000 homes in one section of the city, 100,000 homes in another section, and then 250,000 homes in another section.

The results were different than expected on a response rate per thousand.

The 100,000 mailing brought more returns per 1,000 than the 50,000.

The 250,000 mailing brought more returns per 1,000 than the 100,000.

In other words, results per thousand INCREASED as the mailings became larger. Here's why: When you advertise to a few people they read what you have to say and either act on it or very soon forget all about it. When you advertise something to practically everybody in a community, people not only individually read what you have to say but they talk about it to other people – and that is what gets results.

The same principle works in personal selling. The more people you ask to buy the better your closing ratio will be.

Here is another good example making more calls. A friend of mine told me about the time he was a national sales manager for a pharmaceutical company and had the challenge of getting his sales people to make more calls.

While thinking about how to approach his sales team with the challenge of making more calls he phoned one of his friends, an up and coming physician who worked for a new service that makes house calls on patients, to ask his opinion about one of the products he was selling. When the doctor came to the phone he said "I just can't talk to you now, call me at nine-thirty tonight." When the sales manager telephoned that night the doctor apologized. "I'm sorry I couldn't talk to you today, it's just one of my regular days – I made house calls on thirty-four patients, had an hour and a half of consultation at my office and delivered two babies."

My friend said he was not at a loss for an interesting opening statement when he began his speech at their national sales meeting.

Are you familiar with The Rule of Seven? It started back in Hollywood during the Great Depression, when people had limited money and shouldn't have been spending it on movies when they had so many other, more pressing needs. The marketing folks discovered that to motivate a person to attend a show, they had to hit those people at least 7 times in a short period of time. Then they showed up at the box office. We've got to do the same thing with our personal selling. When you target a new account, try making seven calls with short intervals in between.

"Familiarity breeds contempt," is commonly accepted, but it is not true. A study conducted in 1982 published in the Journal of Experimental Social Psychology, by R. L. Moreland and R. B. Zajonc, said that repeated exposure to any stimulus leads to a greater appreciation and liking. This is great news for us in sales and marketing. Exposure and repetition can only increase sales.

As a sales person there are several things you can do on the personal level that will make you unique. The first thing you can do is show up either in person, on the phone, in the mail or in their email inbox.

How many contacts does it take to make a sale?

These numbers are the most important sales statistics you will ever read and they can have a huge impact on your business...

48% of sales people never follow up with a customer

25% make a second contact and stop

12% only make three contacts and stop

10% make more than three contacts

With those numbers in mind... here's how you can double or triple your results... make at least 12 contacts before you give up. Here's why.

2% of sales are made on the first contact

3% are made on the second contact

5% are made on the third contact

10% are made on the fourth contact

80% are made on the 5th to 12th contact

Make the connection

I just met the future CEO, President or a guy that is going to be the most amazing manager, sales manager or customer service manager you will ever know!

This guy has restored my faith in the younger generation who are accused of not being able to communicate. They are told they don't know how to interact because all they do is text each other.

No matter how long you have been in sales or management this young man has a lesson for all of us who are trying to increase the level of customer service or get our customers to buy more of our products and services.

I'm not even sure the young man realized the significance of what he did. This small act, if you became infected with, would not only turn your sales around, if everybody did it, the whole economy could turn around.

Most of us are walking around in a daze. We've got our head buried in the sand and we don't even know what's going on around us. We are going through our day saying "why me?" We are worried about being laid off, not being able to pay our bills, losing our customers. "Everything was going so good a few years ago, but now, everything is falling apart."

Well, this young night clerk in the La Quinta Inn demonstrated to me that if you go the extra mile with a little bit of sincere attention you can go from "why me" to "why not me?"

Here's what he did to make such an impression.

When I checked in he said: "Welcome Mr. Oros, I see you are a motivational speaker!"

You might be wondering what the big deal is?

Here's the big deal. My email address is Bob@BobOros.com. This young man took the initiative to look up my website to see what I do. That small, seemingly insignificant jester has NEVER been done by any of the thousands of hotels I have stayed in. None of the Hiltons, Hyatt's or Crown Plazas where I use my email address for my confirmation have ever felt that my business was important enough, or they were at least a little curious about one of their customers.

Let's compare that with my bank.

They just started a new program. When you go through the drive through they remind you that your car payment is due!

Not: "Hello Mr. Oros, I hope you're having a great day!"

All they say is: "Do you know your car payment is due?"

Here was my reply: "How stupid do you think I am? Of course I know my car payment is due and it will be paid Friday, which is well within the terms of the loan!"

Why not put a little note on my account that said: "Bob Oros. Loyal customer since 1988. Over 3 million dollars deposited. Motivational speaker. Ask advice on how to get motivated.

EVERYBODY is hungry for a little attention!

What do you know about your customers? Have you been to their website? Have you read their advertisements?

It's like everybody is going around building thousands of shallow, meaningless relationships on Twitter and MySpace rather than paying attention to the person right in front of you!

When that young man looked me in the eye, welcomed me, and gave me the ultimate compliment of a little attention, he made the sale. That personal attention meant more to me than all the "tweets" on Twitter will EVER mean!

I am on an airplane on my way to do a seminar where I will be staying for three nights. Am I staying at the Hyatt? Nope. Am I staying at the Hilton? Nope. I am staying at the La Quinta to remind myself that when I meet with my customers and give my speech, to gather all the information I can, be sincerely interested in them - and pay attention!

The best advice I can give you is to get your head out of the electronic sand. Use all your "e" stuff to simplify your life. Use it as an amazing tool to collect information, communicate, learn and keep records.

But when it comes to customer service, selling, motivating your staff or building your relationships there is nothing more effective than a smile, the sound of your voice, eye contact, a handshake, a meaningful conversation and a little sincere attention to seal the deal.

Lose the "power tie"

I knew it was going to be a bad day when the VP of sales made a special trip to be with me on a new account call. On the way to the appointment the questions kept coming on.

~ What are you going to present?

~ What are you going to demo?

~ Where is your point of sale?

~ Where are your product books?

~ Why don't you invest in a nicer looking suit?

~ You need to be wearing a "power tie!"

As soon as we got into the customer's office my VP dominated the conversation. The prospect stopped him in mid sentence, called in a young man from outside the office and wrote a note on a piece of paper. The young man read the note, and then suggested that my VP join him. I was to remain in the office.

When they left the room, the customer started to loosen up. He started to tell me about his company, what his needs were and what results he would like to achieve. He suggested that we have a second meeting to discuss things in more detail.

The note the customer handed to the young man said: "Get the guy wearing the 'power tie' out of my office! Leave the other man here with me. I believe he can help us with those ideas we were discussing a few weeks ago."

What goes around

You wouldn't come right out and tell your customers to "take a hike" would you?

Well, by not talking with your customers one-on-one and fully explaining to them why you have shut off their credit and raised their prices, you might as well.

Let me explain.

The hardest thing for a person to do is face a customer and give them some news they may not want to hear. It takes real guts. It is easier to just let things take care of themselves.

For example.

If you don't call a customer and tell them they are going to be on COD, they will find out when the delivery comes. Right? If you have to raise their prices at the same time because they owe you money, so be it. Right?

Don't go and see them. Don't call them. Let the order go out COD. Raise their prices. Go hide under a rock. Here's the result of this cowardly way of doing business.

Customer calls YOU and leaves the following voice mail.

"What the hell are you doing sending this order in COD? I just paid you some money and I assumed I was going to get this order. I NEED it for today's business! And you jacked up these prices! What are you trying to do to me? The next time you or anyone from your company steps foot in my business you better be wearing a bullet proof vest! I will come out of this. My situation is only temporary. And when I do turn it around you can believe I will NEVER buy from your company. And if I ever end up working for someone else, you can believe I will do everything in my power to make sure we don't do business with the likes of you!"

Your long term reputation in your market is at stake. People DON'T FORGET how you treated them. And to tell your customers to "take a hike" without a little respect will come back to you. In the long run, they will be the ones telling YOU to TAKE A HIKE. It may be a year, two years, or even 5 years. But dumping a customer without an explanation and burning the bridge is a pretty poor way to run a business. Yet it's being done every day!

I want to challenge you to do it the right way!

Let's say I have been a loyal customer for several years and I get in a little jam. I don't expect you to carry me financially. I don't expect you to give me the same low prices as someone who pays cash or within 7 days.

Here is what I DO expect. I DO expect YOU to have the following conversation with me.

"Mr. Customer, we have to talk about your account. It is getting behind and as much as I appreciate your business, we have to abide by company policy. Starting on your next order it will be necessary to pay COD. I know this is not something you want to hear and believe me, it is not something I want to have to tell you. Also, the special pricing I have been giving you will have to be slightly adjusted. They were based on you paying within the 10 day terms."

(Note: This is not some form letter - this is YOU talking with ME, a customer!)

"I want to keep you as a customer and help you in any way I can within the limits of what I can do. I want to keep our relationship going and see what I can do to help you grow your sales and recover some of your lost business. I know this has been a tough time for you and the lost business is through no fault of your own. I respect and appreciate your situation. I want to keep the door open and work towards re-building your business and re-establishing our business."

That wasn't so bad, was it?

One word sums it up. Reciprocity.

Definition: In-kind positive or negative responses of individuals towards the actions of others. In other words, what goes around comes around.

Service: Help customers build their business

My primary goal is to help my customer become more successful. I am not just selling products and services they can buy from any competitor; I am selling them ideas, consulting services and my personal services. I can proudly say that "I" go with every order and I truly make a difference in their business. While my competitors may be looking at the commission they make, I am more concerned with helping my customer make more money and improve their business. My products and services were created to help my customers solve a problem. My customers buy from me because I am able to convey this helpful approach on every sales call and in every meeting with my customers.

My 4% improvement objective:

_____

_____

_____

_____

_____

_____

What the entire book series will do for you

Buying all 13 books is like buying a library of 13 powerful coaching sessions that will increase every skill necessary for generating business. Once you experience the seemingly effortless improvement you will understand why there is a picture of Ben Franklin on every 100 dollar bill.

You will learn how to improve relationships, improve management skills, be more productive, generate more customers, negotiate better contracts, open new accounts, earn more profits and create more sales! Results most people only dream about! If you are a sales professional or an entrepreneur this is the perfect program to boost your sales and increase your profits.

Ben Franklin's system

In our fast paced business and personal life today it has become increasingly difficult to set aside time for self development and improving your skills. With every spare minute taken up by reading blogs, logging on to Facebook, following people on Twitter, responding to text messages and emails and constantly talking on your cell phone, there seems to be little, if any, time left for learning new skills. Even the quiet time behind the wheel of your car is no longer available with satellite radio and cell phone coverage in every corner of the country.

Even though this seems like a new problem, distractions have been around forever. Two hundred years ago a man by the name of Ben Franklin had the same problem. He concluded that it was not a matter of distractions as much as a matter of focus. He set out to solve the problem and created the most effective system for self improvement ever invented.

Ben Franklin gives credit for all his success and accomplishments to the implementation of this system for the success he sought after. Despite being born into a poor family and only receiving two years of formal schooling, Ben Franklin became a successful printer, scientist, musician, author and one of the founding fathers of the United States. Ben Franklin is considered to have been one of the most persuasive and successful people in the history of the United States. He was a very skilled sales person, marketer, negotiator and copywriter. Skills that every business owner, professional person, manager and marketer should have.

In the year 1723, Ben Franklin, at the age of seventeen, arrived in Philadelphia without a penny to his name. At age 42, he retired, wealthy, the first self made millionaire in the country. Few people, before or since have ever been as successful as Benjamin Franklin. He gave credit for his many inventions and business successes to his system for self improvement he created when he was 20 years old.

The key to Franklin's success was his drive to constantly improve himself and accomplish his ambitions. In order to accomplish his goal, Franklin developed and committed himself to a personal improvement program that consisted of mastering 13 principles.

When he was seventy-nine years old, Benjamin Franklin wrote more about this idea than anything else that ever happened to him in his entire life.   He felt that he owed all his success and happiness to this one thing. Franklin wrote: "I hope, therefore, that some of my descendants may follow the example and reap the benefit."

Since success is developed by performing small and seemingly insignificant acts, you can use this method by reading and putting into practice the 13 skills that will guarantee your success in sales with scientific certainty.

This program takes advantage of Franklin's system and applies it to improving your skills as a sales professional. This program will show you how to dominate your market by first dominating yourself. By focusing on the 13 skills that make up a highly effective and successful sales professional. As these skills are improved your results and sales increases will also show a dramatic improvement.

The goal of going through the program the first time is to increase each skill by only four percent. With the accomplishment of this small improvement in each skill or attitude your overall improvement will be 52%. Those are results most people only dream about. However, you can accomplish this by investing as little as 45 minutes once a week reading one book and then focusing on improving the single skill during the rest of the week. The second week by reading the second book and focusing on that single skill during the week and so on until all 13 weeks are completed.

You can write the single word on the back of your business card and tape it to your dash board as a reminder. You can put this one word on your smart phone as a reminder as well as on your email signature, your Facebook page or you can even have something worthwhile to tweet about. One word, one week, one skill, one "I am" statement, 4% improvement objective and your subconscious mind will receive the message through all the clutter and act on it.

After the first time through the process you can do as Ben Franklin suggests and go through the program a second, third and fourth time. Get your whole sales team on the same page at the same time and you will experience a whirlwind of new excitement and new business. Or get a like minded colleague and join forces with accountability and focus.

Achieve a 52% improvement

Using Franklin's scientific program for learning your objective is to improve 4% in each area over 13 weeks.

1. Attitude Define what you want and go after it.
2. Respect Earn respect-no more comfort zone.
3. Service Help customers build their business.
4. Urgency Be enthusiastic get things done now.
5. Confidence Remove restrictions and limitations.
6. Persistence Keep going and never give up.
7. Planning Get big results by setting big goals.
8. Questions Ask questions that make the sale.
9. Attention Get attention with irresistible offers.
10. Presenting Give reasons why they should buy.
11. Objections Remove every roadblock to the sale.
12. Closing Ask for the order and get paid.
13. Follow up Remove all hope for competitors.

ATTITUDE
Define what you want and go after it

CONFIDENCE

PRESENTING
Give reasons why they should buy

RESPECT
Earn respect by being an expert

PERSISTENCE

OBJECTIONS
Remove every roadblock to the sale

SERVICE
Help customers build their business

Ben Franklin's little known scientific

PLANNING

CLOSING
Ask for the order and get paid

Ben Franklin's little known scientific
formula improves selling skills 52%

QUESTIONS

URGENCY
Be enthusiastic get things done now

Ben Franklin's little known scientific
formula improves selling skills 52%

ATTENTION
Make irresistible compelling offers

Ben Franklin's little known scientific
formula improves selling skills 52%

FOLLOW UP
Remove all hope for competitors

Ben Franklin's little known scientific
formula improves selling skills 52%

Bob Oros

Bob Oros

Bob Oros

54

About the author Bob Oros (BobOros.com),

Bob Oros has been a full time speaker and author since 1992 with over 2,000 speaking engagements in all 50 states and several international locations as well as the author of 21 books on sales. Prior to starting his speaking career, Bob served six years in the US Navy as a Communications Specialist and then worked his way from a street sales person to the position of National Sales Manager for a Fortune 200 company.

CSP Award: Bob was awarded the designation of Certified Speaking Professional (CSP) by the National Speakers Association and the International Federation for Professional Speakers. Fewer than 10% of all speakers worldwide qualify for this award.

PWA Member: Bob is a member of the Professional Writers Alliance.

www.ingramcontent.com/pod-product-compliance
Lightning Source LLC
Chambersburg PA
CBHW072248170526
45158CB00003BA/1034